Sweet Dreams Indiana

Adriane Doherty • **Anastasiia Kuusk**

Rubber Ducky Press
Carmel, IN

The sun rises as eager eyes open up to a new morning. We are going to explore Indiana searching for adventure.

Let's take a walk along the canal in downtown Indianapolis. We stop for a visit at the Indiana State Museum. There we learn about the history of Indiana.

Engines rooooaaarrr at the Indianapolis Motor Speedway. The cars race around the track as we cheer for our favorite driver.

At the Indianapolis
Zoo, the orangutans
are happily hanging,
climbing, and swinging
from their ropes. There
are so many friendly
faces at the zoo.

A hot air balloon floats high in the sky above Conner Prairie. See Pioneer Village and the horse and wagon below!

The sandy beaches at Indiana Dunes are bursting with excitement. Sailboats are sailing, seagulls are flying, and we are building sandcastles.

The magical carousel ride
welcomes all for a day of fun!

At the local bookstore in Butler-Tarkington, storytime begins. It is my favorite part of the day.

As we head to the Covered Bridge Festival, we see river otters playing. It looks like a game of tag!

The Underground Railroad in Fountain City is where Levi Coffin helped nearly 2,000 slaves to freedom. Levi and his family made a very special mark in history.

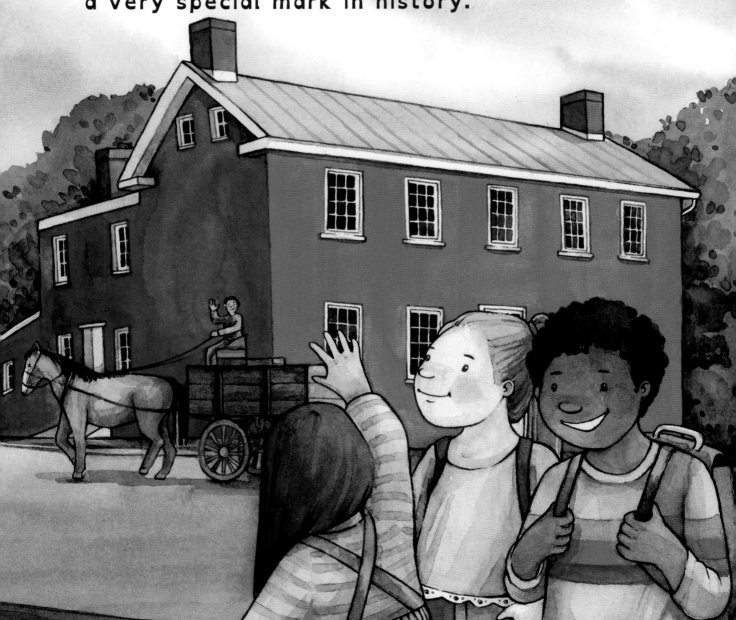

On the Ohio River in Madison,
we watch the steamboat pass by
before enjoying a stroll down
Main Street. First, we stop at
the bookstore, then it's time for
some ice cream! Yum!

After a fun day of paddling the river in Fort Wayne, we head over to Science Central. The many hands-on exhibits show us how fun science can be.

It's a sunny day and families are walking along the Ohio River. We always appreciate our time together.

The sights and sounds of downtown Evansville are full of life!

Near Lafayette in Battle Ground, Indiana we visit Tippecanoe Battlefield and Museum.

Across the street from kidscommons Museum in Columbus, we visit an amazing suspended playground. We climb, play, and meet lots of new friends!

The St. Joseph River in South Bend is home to many interesting places including the Studebaker National Museum. The founder started as a blacksmith and wagonmaker!

We walk through
River Lights Plaza.
It's a beautiful
starry evening.

Sweet dreams,
South Bend!

It's nighttime as the fireflies light up the park. It's time to say goodbye to the rolling hills of Brown County State Park.

Sweet dreams, fireflies.

Sweet dreams, park!

We finish the day
back in downtown
Indianapolis to look
at the Circle of
Lights.

Sweet dreams,
little one.

Sweet dreams,
Circle of Lights!

After a day of exploring, we are warm, cozy, and ready for a bedtime story.

Sweet dreams, explorers!

Wow, what a busy day!

I wonder what we'll do tomorrow?

Sweet dreams, Indiana.

Sweet dreams, everyone!

Where in Indiana did we go today?

* Featured Indianapolis Activities:

Indianapolis Canal Walk • Indiana State Museum

Indianapolis Motor Speedway • Indianapolis Zoo

Indianapolis Children's Museum • Kids Ink Bookstore

Monument Circle

Author Biography:

Born and raised in Indiana, author Adriane Doherty has traveled all across the great Hoosier state. Her love of books and desire to help young minds grow inspired her to write, and now she aims to educate them on the value of the communities where they live and visit. Her other adventures can be found in other *Sweet Dreams* editions and her ABC collection.

Other Rubber Ducky Press Titles You May Enjoy:

ABC Christmas • ABC Kentucky • ABC Michigan • ABC Pennsylvania • ABC Ohio ABC Texas • ABC Yellowstone • Sweet Dreams Chicago • Sweet Dreams Ohio • Sweet Dreams Chesapeake Bay

Follow us on Instagram
@rubberduckypress

Find coloring pages at
rubberduckypress.com

Indiana Dunes National Park

South Bend

Fort Wayne

Battle Ground

Parke County

Conner Prairie

Fountain City

☆ Indianapolis*

Columbus

Brown County State Park

Madison

Evansville